The Sayi

THE SAYINGS OF THE GREAT RELIGIOUS LEADERS

Editor: Andrew Linzey

The Sayings of Jesus

Selected by Andrew Linzey
Director of the Centre for the Study of Theology in the
University of Essex

The Sayings of Moses

Selected by Dan Cohn-Sherbok
University Lecturer in Jewish Theology in the University of
Kent

The Sayings of Muhammad

Selected and Translated by Neal Robinson
Lecturer in Religious Studies in the Cheltenham and
Gloucester College of Higher Education

The Sayings of the Buddha

Selected by Geoffrey Parrinder
Emeritus Professor of Comparative Study of Religions in
the University of London, King's College

The Sayings of

JESUS

selected by

ANDREW LINZEY

DUCKWORTH

First published in 1991 by
Gerald Duckworth & Co. Ltd.
The Old Piano Factory
43 Gloucester Crescent, London NW1 7DY

Introduction and editorial arrangement
© 1991 by Andrew Linzey

ISBN 0 7156 2364 8

British Library Cataloguing in Publication Data
The Sayings of Jesus.
1. Christianity. Doctrines
I. Linzey, Andrew 1952–
232.954

ISBN 0-7156-2364-8

Acknowledgments

I am grateful to the Centre for the Study of Theology in the
University of Essex and in particular to Margaret
Middleton for her kind help in the preparation of the
manuscript. The extracts from the gospels are taken from
the Revised Standard Version of the Bible, © 1952 and 1971,
Division of Christian Education of the Churches of Christ,
USA, and reproduced with permission.

Photoset in North Wales by
Derek Doyle & Associates, Mold, Clwyd
Printed in Great Britain by
Redwood Press Limited, Melksham

Contents

Introduction

The story of Jesus, his life, words, death and resurrection, reverberates through western culture – in art, music, literature, drama, architecture and liturgy. His words have been claimed as a unique source of divine inspiration.

At one level, this claim is puzzling. Few theologians now maintain that Jesus was unique in what he said. Much of it can be paralleled elsewhere. The great commandments to love God and love one's neighbour – so central to his teaching – were of course inherited from Judaism, and some Jewish scholars claim him as an outstanding teacher of pharisaic Judaism. Moreover, as far as teaching is concerned, we have very little of it in the four gospels. What Jesus said falls far short of anything like systematic exposition.

And yet it may be precisely because the words of Jesus are *remembered* words that they continue to attract, astonish or inspire. We know that after the death of Jesus, his sayings were kept in circulation by his disciples through word of mouth. When the first Christians met for worship they broke bread and shared the cup in memory of him. Part of this process also involved bringing into mind the words that Jesus had uttered on one or more occasion. The earliest form of Christian liturgy consisted in remembering: telling the story and sharing the bread. There is little doubt that this creative milieu helped fashion and refashion the sayings of Jesus as they were told over a period of about thirty to sixty years before they were committed to writing. The gospels as we know them are editorial compilations of words recalled – themselves rearranged and developed by the evangelists.

Apart from the canonical and non-canonical gospels, we have no independent access to the historical Jesus. References, such as they are, in other books of the time are unhelpful or oblique. The attempt of more than a century of biblical scholarship to discover the historical Jesus – as distinct from the Christ of faith – must be judged a failure.

We have no sure criterion for telling which sayings derive directly from Jesus' lips and which are the result of community refashioning. The gospels offer us four collections of community memories. There is no Jesus we can envisage outside them.

What seems to have happened is that this process of remembering Jesus – in word and deed – brought his presence alive among them. His original words began to be interpreted in a new light; to the experience of the historical Jesus was added the new experience of Christ risen and alive. As a result the past was brought into the present in such a way that the present was decisively transformed.

To isolate the sayings of Jesus, therefore, from the full recorded remembrance of the community in the four gospels – and especially from the creative experience of worship – is inevitably to play down the momentum that provided the creativity for the remembrance itself. A world and more separates us from the congregations of Antioch and Ephesus. Their memories of Jesus cannot be identical with our own. Attending to the sayings of Jesus in our own time will be a different remembering from that of the first Christians. Remembering is more, much more, than reminiscence.

But before we despair of the hermeneutical impossibility of knowing precisely what Jesus said or of faithfully appropriating his memory, we would do well to grasp the incontestable fact that these sayings do speak – and continue to speak – to generation after generation. Our western world would be a vastly different place without them. They have inspired some of the greatest writers and artists, who in turn have inspired others. They have brought hope to the dying and despairing as well as solace to the wretched. Some have taken Jesus at his word and given away possessions and lived sacrificially among the poor and desolate. Some, inspired by these sayings, have overcome terrible fears and suffered intolerable deprivations for the sake of others and the pursuit of justice. Behind the asperity of Jesus' more uncompromising words, many have sensed the absolute demands of a holy and righteous God.

In short: the experience of millions of Christians, not least in liturgy, prayer and adoration, is that the gulf that separates us from the first-century Christians can be – and is – transcended. The remembering of Jesus continues to be a transformative experience. The gospels embody this continuing claim that 'the words I have spoken to you are spirit and life' (John 6:63).

Even Albert Schweitzer – whose book *The Quest of the Historical Jesus* failed to live up to the promise of its title – was moved to write these concluding lines: 'He comes to us as one unknown, without a name, as of old by the lake side. He came to those men who knew Him not. He speaks to us the same words: "Follow thou me," and sets us to the same task which He has to fulfil for our time. He commands. And to those who obey Him, whether they be wise or simple, He will reveal Himself in the toils, the conflicts, the sufferings which they shall pass through in His fellowship and, as an ineffable mystery, they shall learn in their own experience who He is.'

The exact dating of the gospels is still a contentious issue. Most scholars put the three synoptic gospels (Mark, Matthew and Luke) after AD 70 and John significantly later. It is generally agreed that the synoptic gospels drew from common sources, or improved upon the first gospel (Mark). There are therefore many identical, or almost identical, passages. In this book few repetitions have been included unless there is a significant change of emphasis (for instance, Matthew's exception in the case in divorce in 5:31-32, cf. Mark 10:11-12). In such cases the parallel passages have been placed one after the other.

Commands

Despite Matthew's portrayal of Jesus as the fulfilment of Jewish law (5:17-18), there is a conspicuous absence of detailed prescription in the teaching of Jesus. Possible exceptions include opposition to the common practice of swearing oaths (Matthew 5:33-35) and the upholding of the life-long nature of marriage so that divorce is prohibited (though note the Matthean exception on the grounds of unchastity, 5:31-32; cf. Mark 10:11-12). Generally, however, Jesus is presented as hostile to the perceived legalism of the scribes and pharisees, though many scholars now hold that the poor image of the scribes and pharisees owes much to inter-community conflicts after AD 70. The Sermon on the Mount (Matthew 5-7) does not lay down new ethical law, codes or regulations, rather it illustrates the unconditional demands of a holy God. Thus it is not only wrong to kill your brother, it is equally wrong to insult him (Matthew 5:21-22). Likewise it is not only wrong to commit adultery, it is also wrong to look at a woman lustfully (Matthew 5:27-28). In these ways, Jesus rejects the all too familiar attempt to reduce God's will to a simple set of moral rules. His own summary of the law, namely, love God and love your neighbour, for on them depend 'all the law and the prophets' (Matthew 22:37-40), effectively fulfils the law only in the sense of relativising all other commandments.

*

You shall love the Lord your God with all your heart, and with all your soul, and with all your mind. The second is like it, You shall love your neighbour as yourself. On these two commandments depend all the law and the prophets.   Matthew 22:27-40

You are the light of the world. A city set on a hill cannot be hid. Nor do men light a lamp and put it under a bushel, but on a stand, and it gives light to all in the house. Let your light so shine before men, that they may see your good works and give glory to your Father who is in heaven.
Matthew 5:14-16

If I then, your Lord and Teacher, have washed your feet, you also ought to wash one another's feet. For I have given you an example, that you also should do as I have done to you.
John 13:14-15

If your right eye causes you to sin, pluck it out and throw it away; it is better that you lose one of your members than that your whole body be thrown into hell.
Matthew 5:29

Come to me, all who labour and are heavy laden, and I will give you rest. Take my yoke upon you, and learn from me; for I am gentle and lowly in heart, and you will find rest for your souls. For my yoke is easy, and my burden is light.
Matthew 12:28-30

Blessed are the merciful, for they shall obtain mercy.
Matthew 5:7

He who is not with me is against me, and he who does not gather with me scatters.
Matthew 12:30

Whoever divorces his wife and marries another, commits adultery against her; and if she divorces her husband and marries another, she commits adultery.
Mark 10:11-12

It was also said, 'Whoever divorces his wife, let him give her a certificate of divorce.' But I say to you that every one who divorces his wife, except on the ground of unchastity, makes her an adultress; and whoever marries a divorced woman commits adultery.
Matthew 5:31-32

Every one then who hears these words of mine and does them will be like a wise man who built his house upon the rock; and the rain fell, and the floods came, and the winds blew and beat upon that house, but it did not fall, because it had been founded on the rock. And every one who hears these words of mine and does not do them, will be like a foolish man who built his house upon the sand; and the rain fell, and the floods came, and the winds blew and beat against the house, and it fell; and great was the fall of it.

Matthew 7:24-27

Why do you call me 'Lord, Lord', and not do what I tell you? Every one who comes to me and hears my words and does them, I will show you what he is like: he is like a man building a house, who dug deep, and laid the foundation upon rock; and when a flood arose, the stream broke against that house, and could not shake it, because it had been well built. But he who hears and does not do them is like a man who built a house on the ground without a foundation; against which the stream broke, and immediately it fell, and the ruin of that house was great.

Luke 6:46-49

Again, you have heard that it was said to the men of old, 'You shall not swear falsely, but shall perform to the Lord what you have sworn.' But I say to you, Do not swear at all, either by heaven, for it is the throne of God, or by the earth, for it is his footstool, or by Jerusalem, for it is the city of the great King.

Matthew 5:33-35

Blessed are the peacemakers, for they shall be called sons of God.

Matthew 5:9

All who take the sword will perish by the sword.

Matthew 26:52

Render therefore to Caesar the things that are Caesar's, and to God the things that are God's. Matthew 22:21

The poor you always have with you, but you do not always have me. John 12:8

Have you not read that he who made them from the beginning made them male and female, and said, 'For this reason a man shall leave his father and mother and be joined to his wife, and the two shall become one flesh?' So they are no longer two but one flesh. What therefore God has joined together, let not man put asunder.

Matthew 19:4-6

You therefore must be perfect, as your heavenly Father
is perfect. Matthew 5:48

Blessed are those who hunger and thirst for righteousness,
for they shall be satisfied. Matthew 5:6

For every one who exalts himself will be humbled, and he
who humbles himself will be exalted. Luke 14:11

You have heard that it was said to the men of old, 'You
shall not kill; and whoever kills shall be liable to judgment.'
But I say to you that every one who is angry with his
brother shall be liable to judgment; whoever insults his
brother shall be liable to the council, and whoever says
'You fool!' shall be liable to the hell of fire.
Matthew 5:21-22

Blessed are the pure in heart, for they shall see God.
Matthew 5:8

Remember Lot's wife. Luke 17:32

Are not five sparrows sold for two pennies? And not one of
them is forgotten before God. Luke 12:6

It is written, 'You shall not tempt the Lord your God.'
Matthew 4:7

Blessed are the meek, for they shall inherit the earth.
Matthew 5:5

You have heard that it was said, 'You shall not commit
adultery.' But I say to you that every one who looks at a
woman lustfully has already committed adultery with her
in his heart. Matthew 5:27-28

You have heard that it was said, 'An eye for an eye and a tooth for a tooth.' But I say to you, Do not resist one who is evil. But if any one strikes you on the right cheek, turn to him the other also; and if any one would sue you and take your coat, let him have your cloak as well; and if any one forces you to go one mile, go with him two miles. Give to him who begs from you, and do not refuse him who would borrow from you.
Matthew 5:38-42

Blessed are those who mourn, for they shall be comforted.
Matthew 5:4

Think not that I have come to abolish the law and the prophets; I have come not to abolish them but to fulfil them. For truly, I say to you, till heaven and earth pass away, not an iota, not a dot, will pass from the law until all is accomplished.
Matthew 5:17-18

What comes out of a man is what defiles a man. For within, out of the heart of man, come evil thoughts, fornication, theft, murder, adultery, coveting, wickedness, deceit, licentiousness, envy, slander, pride, foolishness. And these evil things come from within, and they defile a man.
Mark 7:20-23

Hear and understand: not what goes into the mouth defiles a man, but what comes out of the mouth, this defiles a man.
Matthew 15:10-11

Do not lay up for yourselves treasures on earth, where moth and rust consume and where thieves break in and steal, but lay up for yourselves treasure in heaven, where neither moth nor rust consumes and where thieves do not break in and steal. For where your treasure is, there will your heart be also.
Matthew 6:19-21

No one can serve two masters; for either he will hate the one and love the other, or he will be devoted to the one and despise the other. You cannot serve God and mammon.
Matthew 6:24

Therefore I tell you, do not be anxious about your life, what you shall eat or what you shall drink, nor about your body, what you shall put on. Is not life more than food, and the body more than clothing? Look at the birds of the air; they neither sow nor reap nor gather into barns, and yet your heavenly Father feeds them.   Matthew 6:25-26

Whoever receives one such child in my name receives me: but whoever causes one of these little ones who believe in me to sin, it would be better for him to have a great millstone fastened round his neck and to be drowned in the depth of the sea.   Matthew 18:5-6

So have no fear of them; for nothing is covered that will not be revealed or hidden that it will not be known. What I tell you in the dark, utter in the light; and what you hear whispered, proclaim upon the house-tops. And do not fear those who kill the body but cannot kill the soul; rather fear him who can destroy both soul and body in hell.
               Matthew 10:26-28

When it is evening, you say, 'It will be fair weather for the sky is red.' And in the morning, 'It will be stormy today, for the sky is red and threatening.' You know how to interpret the appearance of the sky, but you cannot interpret the signs of the times. An evil and adulterous generation seeks for a sign, but no sign shall be given to it except the sign of Jonah.   Matthew 16:2-4

Do not forbid him [man casting out demons] for he that is not against you is for you.   Luke 9:50

No one puts new wine into old wineskins; if he does, the wine is lost, and so are the skins; but new wine is for fresh skins.   Mark 2:22

[To the sea] Peace! Be still!   Mark 4:39

Take heed, beware of the leaven of the pharisees and the leaven of Herod.   Mark 8:15

[To the unclean spirit] Be silent and come out of him!
               Mark 1:25

Take heed what you hear; the measure you give will be the measure you get, and still more will be given you.

Mark 4:24

The light is with you for a little longer. Walk while you have the light, lest the darkness overtake you; he who walks in the darkness does not know where he goes.

John 12:35

Be merciful, even as your Father is merciful.   Luke 6:36

For to him who has shall more be given, and from him who has not, even what he thinks that he has will be taken away.

Luke 8:18

Do not weep; for she [Jairus' daughter] is not dead but sleeping.

Luke 8:52

Let your loins be girded and your lamps burning, and be like men who are waiting for their master to come home from the marriage feast, so that they may open to him at once when he comes and knocks. Blessed are those servants whom the master finds awake when he comes; truly, I say to you, he will gird himself and have them sit at table, and he will come and serve them.   Luke 12:35-37

[To the pharisees] I tell you if these [Jesus' disciples] were silent, the very stones would cry out.   Luke 19:40

[To the disciples in the upper room after the resurrection] You are witnesses of these things. And behold, I send the promise of my Father upon you; but stay in the city, until you are clothed with power from on high.   Luke 24:48-49

The eye is the lamp of the body. So, if your eye is sound, your whole body will be full of light; and if your eye is not sound, your whole body will be full of darkness. If then the light in you is darkness, how great is the darkness!

Matthew 6:22-23

When they persecute you in one town, flee to the next; for truly, I say to you, you will not have gone through all the towns of Israel, before the Son of man comes.

Matthew 10:23

Why do you transgress the commandment of God for the sake of your tradition? For God commanded, 'Honour your father and your mother,' and 'He who speaks evil of father or mother, let him surely die.' But you say, 'If any one tells his father or his mother, What you would have gained from me is given to God, he need not honour his father.' So, for the sake of your tradition, you have made void the word of God. You hypocrites!   Matthew 14:3-7

You are not to be called rabbi, for you have one teacher, and you are all brethren. And call no man your father on earth, for you have one Father, who is in heaven. Neither be called masters, for you have one master, the Christ. He who is greatest among you shall be your servant; and whoever exalts himself shall be humbled, and whoever humbles himself shall be exalted.   Matthew 23:8-12

Rise, take up your pallet, and walk.   John 5:8

Discipleship

Most scholars do not think that Jesus sought to found a church as such, yet he did create around him a community of twelve men and some women companions, such as Mary Magdalen. The gospels characterise discipleship as nothing less than the sharing of Jesus' own way of costly sacrifice. 'If any man would come after me, let him deny himself and take up his cross and follow me' (Mark 8:35). Such sacrifice involved the renunciation of worldly possessions (Mark 10:21), and the rejection of the primacy of family relations for the sake of the gospel (Mark 3:35). The urgent demands of discipleship meant that even the dead should be left 'to bury their own dead' (Matthew 8:22). Non-retaliation in the face of injury and acceptance of persecution were the hall-marks of true discipleship (Matthew 5:11-12). Most significantly of all, Matthew and Luke envisage a reversal of the usual hierarchical relationships within the Christian community itself. Whereas Gentile rulers lord it over their subjects – 'it shall not be so among you; but whoever would be first among you must be your servant' (Matthew 20:25-28; Luke 22:25-27; cf. John 13:12-17), in principle at least the gospel writers envisage a community dedicated to communal self-sacrifice modelled on the self-giving of Jesus himself.

*

Take nothing for your journey, no staff, nor bag, nor bread, nor money; and do not have two tunics. And whatever house you enter, stay there, and from there depart. And wherever they do not receive you, when you leave that town shake off the dust from your feet as a testimony against them.   Luke 9:3-5

All authority in heaven and on earth has been given to me. Go therefore and make disciples of all nations, baptizing them in the name of the Father and of the Son and of the Holy Spirit, teaching them to observe all that I have commanded you; and lo, I am with you always to the close of the age.   Matthew 28:18-20

If you continue in my word, you are truly my disciples, and you will know the truth, and the truth will make you free.
                                    John 8:31-32

Follow me, and I will make you fishers of men.
                                    Matthew 4:19

Go into all the world and preach the gospel to the whole creation. He who believes and is baptized will be saved; but he who does not believe will be condemned.
                                    Mark 16:15-16

Blessed are you when men revile you and persecute you and utter all kinds of evil against you falsely on my account. Rejoice and be glad, for your reward is great in heaven, for so men persecuted the prophets who were before you.   Matthew 5:11-12

Whoever does the will of God is my brother, and sister, and mother.   Mark 3:35

You are the salt of the earth; but if salt has lost its taste, how shall its saltness be restored? It is no longer good for anything except to be thrown out and trodden under foot by men.   Matthew 5:13

You know that the rulers of the Gentiles lord it over them, and their great men exercise authority over them. It shall not be so among you; but whoever would be great among you must be your servant, and whoever would be first among you must be your slave; even as the Son of man came not to be served but to serve, and to give his life as a ransom for many.   Matthew 20:25-28

If any one would be first, he must be last of all and servant of all.   Mark 9:35

The harvest is plentiful, but the labourers are few; pray
therefore the Lord of the harvest to send out labourers into
his harvest.   Matthew 9:37-38

[To Peter] Feed my sheep.   John 21:17

[To the twelve disciples] Go nowhere among the Gentiles,
and enter no town of the Samaritans, but go rather to the
lost sheep of the house of Israel.   Matthew 10:5-6

Follow me, and leave the dead to bury their own dead.
                                                Matthew 8:22

You lack one thing; go, sell what you have, and give to the
poor, and you will have treasure in heaven; and come,
follow me.   Mark 10:21

Behold, I send you out as sheep in the midst of wolves; so
be wise as serpents and innocent as doves.
                                                Matthew 10:16

As you enter the house, salute it. And if the house is
worthy, let your peace come upon it; but if it is not worthy,
let your peace return to you. And if any one will not receive
you or listen to your words, shake off the dust from your
feet as you leave that house or town. Truly, I say to you, it
shall be more tolerable on the day of judgment for the land
of Sodom and Gomorrah than for that town.
                                                Matthew 10:12-15

The scribes and the pharisees sit on Moses' seat; so practise
and observe whatever they tell you, but not what they do;
for they preach, but do not practise. They bind heavy
burdens, hard to bear, and lay them on men's shoulders;
but they themselves will not move them with their finger.
                                                Matthew 23:2-4

If any man would come after me, let him deny himself and
take up his cross and follow me. For whoever would save
his life will lose it; and whoever loses his life for my sake
and the gospel's will save it.   Mark 8:34-35

Behold, I have given you authority to tread upon serpents and scorpions, and over all the power of the enemy; and nothing shall hurt you. Luke 10:19

For truly, I say to you, whoever gives you a cup of water to drink because you bear the name of Christ, will by no means lose his reward. Mark 9:41

Whoever would save his life will lose it, and whoever loses his life for my sake will find it. For what will it profit a man, if he gains the whole world and forfeits his life?
Matthew 16:25-26

Every one to whom much is given, of him will much be required; and of him to whom men commit much they will demand the more. Luke 12:48

If you would be perfect, go, sell what you possess and give to the poor, and you will have treasure in heaven; and come, follow me. Matthew 19:21

Truly I say to you, many prophets and righteous men longed to see what you see, and did not see it, and to hear what you hear, and did not hear it. Matthew 13:17

He who receives a prophet because he is a prophet shall receive a prophet's reward, and he who receives a righteous man shall receive a righteous man's reward. And whoever gives to one of these little ones even a cup of cold water because he is a disciple, truly, I say to you, he shall not lose his reward. Matthew 11:40-42

Do not labour for the food which perishes, but for the food which endures to eternal life, which the Son of man will give to you; for on him has God the Father set his seal.
John 6:27

Peace be with you. As the Father has sent me, even so I send you. John 20:21

[Concerning the failure of Jesus' disciples to fast] Can the wedding guests fast while the bridegroom is with them? As long as they have the bridegroom with them, they cannot fast. The day will come, when the bridegroom is taken away from them, and then they will fast in that day.

Mark 2:19

But take heed to yourselves; for they will deliver you up to councils; and you will be beaten in synagogues; and you will stand before governors and kings for my sake, to bear testimony before them. And the gospel must be preached to all nations. And when they bring you to trial and deliver you up, do not be anxious beforehand what you are to say; but say whatever is given you in that hour, for it is not you who speak, but the Holy Spirit.

Mark 13:9-11

[Concerning Nathanael] Behold, an Israelite indeed, in whom there is no guile!

John 1:47

The wind blows where it wills, and you hear the sound of it, but you do not know whence it comes or whither it goes; so it is with every one who is born of the Spirit.

John 3:8

If any one serves me, he must follow me; and where I am, there shall my servant be also.

John 12:26

No longer do I call you servants, for the servant does not know what his master is doing; but I have called you friends, for all that I have heard from my Father I have made known to you.

John 15:15

As you wish that men would do to you, do so to them.

Luke 6:31

Whoever of you does not renounce all that he has cannot be my disciples.

Luke 14:33

Preach as you go, saying, 'The kingdom of heaven is at hand.' Heal the sick, raise the dead, cleanse lepers, cast out demons.

Matthew 10:7-8

If any one says to you, 'Lo, here is the Christ!' or 'There he is!' do not believe it. For false Christs and false prophets will arise and show great signs and wonders, so as to lead astray, if possible, even the elect. Lo, I have told you beforehand.   Matthew 24:23-24

Prayer

Jesus gives little advice about prayer except that it should be un-hypocritical, devoid of empty phrases and preferably done in secret (Matthew 6:1-8; Mark 12:38-40). The public prayer and self-regarding rituals of the scribes and pharisees are treated with scorn (Matthew 6:16-18). The prayer recommended by Jesus is simple and almost entirely petitionary in character (Matthew 6:9-13). Jesus' own prayer takes place before or after periods of public ministry; he withdraws to pray and almost always prays alone. In John's gospel, Jesus prays that his disciples may be kept in the truth, protected from evil, and 'may all be one … so that the world may believe' (17:6-21).

*

The hour is coming, and now is, when the true worshippers will worship the Father in spirit and truth, for such the Father seeks to worship him. God is spirit, and those who worship him must worship in spirit and truth.
John 4:23-24

Begone, Satan! for it is written, 'You shall worship the Lord your God and him only shall you serve'.
Matthew 4:10

Beware of the scribes, who like to go about in long robes, and to have salutations in the market places and the best seats in the synagogues and the places of honour at feasts, who devour widows' houses and for a pretence make long prayers.
Mark 12:38-40

And when you pray, you must not be like the hypocrites; for they love to stand and pray in the synagogues and at the street corners, that they may be seen by men. Truly, I say to you, they have received their reward. But when you pray, go into your room and shut the door and pray to your Father who is in secret; and your Father who sees in secret will reward you.
Matthew 6:5-6

I have manifested thy name to the men whom thou gavest me out of the world; thine they were, and thou gavest them to me, and they have kept thy word. Now they know that everything that thou hast given me is from thee; for I have given them the words which thou gavest me, and they have received them and know in truth that I came from thee; and they have believed that thou didst send me. I am praying for them; I am not praying for the world but for those whom thou hast given me, for they are thine; all mine are thine, and thine are mine, and I am glorified in them.   John 17:6-10

The harvest is plentiful, but the labourers are few; pray therefore the Lord of the harvest to send out labourers into his harvest.   Luke 10:2

Watch and pray that you may not enter into temptation; the spirit indeed is willing, but the flesh is weak.
                                                                    Matthew 26:41

I do not pray that thou shouldst take them out of the world, but that thou shouldst keep them from the evil one.
                                                                    John 17:15

And in praying do not heap up empty phrases as the Gentiles do; for they think that they will be heard for their many words. Do not be like them, for your Father knows what you need before you ask him.   Matthew 6:7-8

I do not pray for these only, but also for those who believe in me through their word, that they may all be one; even as thou, Father, art in me, and I in thee, that they also may be in us, so that the world may believe that thou hast sent me.   John 17:20-21

Pray then like this: Our Father who art in heaven, hallowed be thy name. Thy kingdom come, thy will be done, on earth as it is in heaven. Give us this day our daily bread; and forgive us our debts, as we also have forgiven our debtors; and lead us not into temptation, but deliver us from evil.   Matthew 6:9-13

And when you fast, do not look dismal, like the hypocrites, for they disfigure their faces that their fasting may be seen by men. Truly, I say to you, they have received their reward. But when you fast, anoint your head and wash your face, that your fasting may not be seen by men but by your Father who is in secret; and your Father who sees in secret will reward you. Matthew 6:16-18

This kind [of spirit] cannot be driven out by anything but prayer. Mark 9:29

And whatever you ask in prayer, you will receive, if you have faith. Matthew 21:22

My Father, if it be possible, let this cup pass from me; nevertheless, not as I will, but as thou wilt.

Matthew 26:39

It is written, 'My house shall be called a house of prayer'; but you make it a den of robbers. Matthew 21:13

Beware of practising your piety before men in order to be seen by them; for then you will have no reward from your Father who is in heaven. Matthew 6:1

Pray that it may not happen in winter. For in those days there will be such tribulation as has not been from the beginning of the creation which God created until now, and never will be. Mark 13:18-19

[To the disciples] My soul is very sorrowful, even to death; remain here, and watch. Mark 14:34

Truly, truly, I say to you, we speak of what we know, and bear witness to what we have seen; but you do not receive our testimony. If I have told you earthly things and you do not believe, how can you believe if I tell you heavenly things? John 3:11-12

I will pray the Father, and he will give you another Counsellor, to be with you for ever, even the Spirit of truth, whom the world cannot receive, because it neither sees him nor knows him; you know him, for he dwells with you, and will be in you. John 14:16-17

But watch at all times, praying that you may have strength to escape all these things [during the time of judgment] that will take place, and to stand before the Son of man.
Luke 21:36

When you give alms, do not let your left hand know what your right hand is doing, so that your alms may be in secret; and your Father who sees in secret will reward you.
Matthew 6:3-4

Where two or three are gathered in my name, there am I in the midst of them.   Matthew 18:20

[To the chief priests and scribes] Have you never read, 'Out of the mouths of babes and sucklings thou hast brought perfect praise'?   Matthew 21:16

Forgiveness

As they reflected upon the life and work of Jesus, the early Christians came to see him as the embodiment of the forgiveness of God. Jesus had particular sympathy for the outcast, the diseased, the poor and the sinful. A 'friend of tax collectors and sinners' was the reproach of his enemies (Luke 7:33-34). When asked to judge the woman caught in adultery (a sin for which stoning was prescribed), he refuses to condemn her publicly and insists that only those who are without sin should cast stones (John 8:7). Similarly the harlot who loves much is readily forgiven (Luke 7:44-47), and the sins of the paralytic are forgiven so that immediate healing results (Mark 2:8-9). Jesus is prepared to forgive even those who crucify him (Luke 23:34). 'I came not to call the righteous, but sinners' (Matthew 9:13) summarises the orientation of his ministry. The sayings appear divided on the question of whether forgiveness should be unconditional. On the one hand, the disciples are admonished to forgive 'seventy times seven' (Matthew 18:22), that is, illimitably without condition, while, on the other, divine forgiveness is seen as conditional upon us forgiving others (Matthew 6:14-15). Much discussion has been engendered by the reference to 'the blasphemy against the Spirit' which 'will not be forgiven' (Matthew 12:31; Mark 3:28-29). Since the Spirit is itself the source of divine healing and forgiveness, the most satisfying interpretation is that the only unforgivable sin is lack of forgiveness.

*

Do you see this woman? I entered your house, you gave me no water for my feet, but she has wet my feet with her tears and wiped them with her hair. You gave me no kiss, but from the time I came in she has not ceased to kiss my feet. You did not anoint my head with oil, but she has anointed my feet with ointment. Therefore I tell you, her sins, which are many, are forgiven, for she loved much; but he who is forgiven little, loves little. Luke 7:44-47

Let him who is without sin among you be the first to throw a stone at her [woman caught in adultery]. John 8:7

[To the paralytic] My son, your sins are forgiven.
Mark 2:5

Thus it is written, that the Christ should suffer and on the third day rise from the dead, and that repentance and forgiveness of sins should be preached in his name to all nations, beginning from Jerusalem. Luke 24:46-47

For John the Baptist has come eating no bread and drinking no wine; and you say, 'He has a demon'. The Son of man has come eating and drinking; and you say, 'Behold a glutton and a drunkard, a friend of tax collectors and sinners!' Luke 7:33-34

Neither do I condemn you [woman caught in adultery]; go, and do not sin again. John 8:11

I tell you, whatever you ask in prayer, believe that you have received it, and it will be yours. And whenever you stand praying, forgive, if you have anything against any one; so that your Father also who is in heaven may forgive you your trespasses. Mark 11:24-26

For if you forgive men their trespasses, your heavenly Father also will forgive you; but if you do not forgive men their trespasses, neither will your Father forgive your trespasses. Matthew 6:14-15

Father, forgive them; for they know not what they do.
Luke 23:34

Those who are well have no need of a physician, but those who are sick. Go and learn what this means, 'I desire mercy and not sacrifice'. For I came not to call the righteous, but sinners.
Matthew 9:12-13

I have not come to call the righteous, but sinners to repentance.
Luke 5:32

Why do you question thus in your hearts? Which is easier, to say to the paralytic, 'Your sins are forgiven', or to say 'Rise, take up your pallet and walk'?
Mark 2:8-9

Receive the Holy Spirit. If you forgive the sins of any, they are forgiven; if you retain the sins of any, they are retained.
John 20:23

I do not say to you seven times [forgive your brother] but seventy times seven.
Matthew 18:22

If your brother sins, rebuke him, and if he repents, forgive him; and if he sins against you seven times in the day, and turns to you seven times, and says, 'I repent', you must forgive him.
Luke 17:3-4

I tell you, there will be more joy in heaven over one sinner who repents than over ninety-nine righteous persons who need no repentance.
Luke 15:7

I tell you, there is joy before the angels of God over one sinner who repents.
Luke 15:10

Truly, I say to you, all sins will be forgiven the sons of men, and whatever blasphemies they utter: but whoever blasphemes against the Holy Spirit never has forgiveness, but is guilty of an eternal sin.
Mark 3:28-29

Therefore I tell you, every sin and blasphemy will be forgiven men, but the blasphemy against the Spirit will not be forgiven.
Matthew 12:31

[To the man cleansed from demons] Go home to your friends, and tell them how much the Lord has done for you and how he has had mercy on you.   Mark 5:19

So also my heavenly Father will do to you [fail to forgive] if you do not forgive your brother from your heart.

Matthew 18:35

Kingdom

The frequent references to the 'kingdom' found in the
synoptic gospels (Matthew, Mark and Luke) are almost
wholly absent from John. Understanding precisely what
the kingdom may have meant for Jesus and each of the
evangelists is notoriously difficult. Perhaps we should say
that the kingdom represents the rule or reign of God
breaking into human history, but there is no coherent
picture within the gospels. Jesus begins his ministry by
announcing that the kingdom is 'at hand' (Mark 1:5;
Matthew 4:17) and that repentance – meaning a turning to
the living God – is essential. Most scholars interpret the
kingdom eschatologically, that is, as referring to God's
future action in human affairs, yet there appear to be a
variety of understandings within the gospels. The reign of
God is illustrated in the many parables of growth and
discovery (Mark 4:26-29; Matthew 13:31-32; 45-46, etc.).
The righteousness of his disciples must exceed that of the
scribes and pharisees if they are to be fit for the kingdom
(Matthew 5:20), and yet those who are 'poor in spirit' –
knowing their need of God – already possess the kingdom
of heaven (Matthew 5:3). Luke seems to suggest that the
kingdom has already entered human history and 'is in the
midst of you' (17:20-21).

*

To you has been given the secret of the kingdom of God,
but for those outside everything is in parables; so that they
may indeed see but not perceive, and may indeed hear but
not understand; lest they should turn again and be
forgiven.   Mark 4:11-12

To you it has been given to know the secrets of the
kingdom of God; but for others they are in parables, so that
seeing they may not see, and hearing they may not
understand.   Luke 8:10

The time is fulfilled, and the kingdom of God is at hand;
repent, and believe in the gospel.   Mark 1:15

Repent, for the kingdom of heaven is at hand.
                                                Matthew 4:17

Truly, truly, I say to you, unless one is born of water and
the Spirit, he cannot enter the kingdom of God. That which
is born of the flesh is flesh, and that which is born of the
Spirit is spirit.   John 3:5-6

Blessed are the poor in spirit, for theirs is the kingdom of
heaven.   Matthew 5:3

Whenever you enter a town and they receive you, eat what
is set before you; heal the sick in it and say to them, 'The
kingdom of God has come near to you.'   Luke 10:8-9

Blessed are those who are persecuted for righteousness'
sake, for theirs is the kingdom of heaven.   Matthew 5:10

Leave the dead to bury their own dead; but as for you, go
and proclaim the kingdom of God.   Luke 9:60

I tell you, you are Peter, and on this rock I will build my
church, and the powers of death shall not prevail against it.
I will give you the keys of the kingdom of heaven, and
whatever you bind on earth shall be bound in heaven, and
whatever you loose on earth shall be loosed in
heaven.   Matthew 16:18-19

My kingship is not of this world; if my kingship were of
this world, my servants would fight, that I might not be
handed over to the Jews; but my kingship is not from the
world.   John 18:36

The kingdom of God is not coming with signs to be observed; nor will they say, 'Lo, here it is!' or 'There!' for behold, the kingdom of God is in the midst of you.

Luke 17:20-21

Fear not, little flock, for it is your Father's good pleasure to give you the kingdom. Sell your possessions, and give alms; provide yourselves with purses that do not grow old, with a treasure in the heavens that does not fail, where no thief approaches and no moth destroys. For where your treasure is, there will your heart be also.   Luke 12:32-34

Unless your righteousness exceeds that of the scribes and pharisees, you will never enter the kingdom of heaven.

Matthew 5:20

Truly, I say to you, there are some standing here who will not taste death before they see that the kingdom of God has come with power.   Mark 9:1

No one who puts his hand to the plough and looks back is fit for the kingdom of God.   Luke 9:62

Truly, I say to you, unless you turn and become like children, you will never enter the kingdom of heaven. Whoever humbles himself like this child, he is the greatest in the kingdom of heaven.   Matthew 18:3-4

To what shall I compare the kingdom of God? It is like leaven which a woman took and hid in three measures of flour, till it was all leavened.   Luke 13:20-21

Not every one who says to me, 'Lord, Lord' shall enter the kingdom of heaven, but he who does the will of my Father who is in heaven.   Matthew 7:21

I have earnestly desired to eat this passover with you before I suffer; for I tell you I shall not eat it until it is fulfilled in the kingdom of God.   Luke 22:15-16

Truly, I say to you, among those born of women there has risen no one greater than John the Baptist; yet he who is least in the kingdom of heaven is greater than he.

Matthew 11:11

Truly, I say to you, it will be hard for a rich man to enter the kingdom of heaven. Again I tell you, it is easier for a camel to go through the eye of a needle than for a rich man to enter the kingdom of God.

Matthew 19:23-24

Truly, I say to you, I shall not drink again of the fruit of the vine until that day when I drink it new in the kingdom of God.

Mark 14:25

Truly, I say to you, whoever does not receive the kingdom of God like a child shall not enter it.

Mark 10:15

The kingdom of God is as if a man should scatter seed upon the ground, and should sleep and rise night and day, and the seed should sprout and grow, he knows not how. The earth produces of itself, first the blade, then the ear, then the full grain in the ear. But when the grain is ripe, at once he puts in the sickle, because the harvest has come.

Mark 4:26-29

The kingdom of heaven is like a grain of mustard seed which a man took and sowed in his field; it is the smallest of all seeds, but when it has grown it is the greatest of shrubs and becomes a tree, so that the birds of the air come and make nests in its branches.

Matthew 13:31-32

The kingdom of heaven is like treasure hidden in a field, which a man found and covered up; then in his joy he goes and sells all that he has and buys that field.

Matthew 13:44

The kingdom of heaven is like a merchant in search of fine pearls, who, on finding one pearl of great value, went and sold all that he had and bought it.

Matthew 13:45-46

From the days of John the Baptist until now the kingdom of heaven has suffered violence, and men of violence take it by force. For all the prophets and the law prophesied until John; and if you are willing to accept it, he is Elijah who is to come. He who has ears to hear, let him hear.

Matthew 11:12-14

[To the claim that Jesus cast out demons by the power of Beelzebub] How can Satan cast out Satan? If a kingdom is divided against itself, that kingdom cannot stand. And if Satan has risen up against himself and is divided, he cannot stand but is coming to an end.   Mark 3:24-26

[To the scribe who answered wisely] You are not far from the kingdom of God.   Mark 12:34

Let the children come to me, do not hinder them; for to such belongs the kingdom of God.   Mark 10:14

Look at the fig tree, and all the trees; as soon as they come out in leaf, you see for yourselves and know that the summer is already near. So also, when you see these things [tribulations] taking place, you know that the kingdom of God is near.   Luke 21:29-32

You are those who have continued with me in my trials; and I assign to you, as my Father assigned to me, a kingdom, that you may eat and drink at my table in my kingdom, and sit on thrones judging the twelve tribes of Israel.   Luke 22:28-30

Every scribe who has been trained for the kingdom of heaven is like a householder who brings out of his treasure what is new and what is old.   Matthew 13:51-2

Not all men can receive this saying, but only those to whom it is given. For there are eunuchs who have been so from birth, and there are eunuchs who have been made eunuchs by men, and there are eunuchs who have made themselves eunuchs for the sake of the kingdom of heaven. He who is able to receive this, let him receive it.

Matthew 19:11-12

[To the chief priests and the elders] Truly, I say to you, the tax collectors and the harlots go into the Kingdom of God before you. For John [the Baptist] came to you in the way of righteousness, and you did not believe him, but the tax collectors and the harlots believed him; and even when you saw it, you did not afterward repent and believe him.   Matthew 21:31-32

Faith

In all the gospels, faith is presented as the key to healing and salvation. The invincibility of faith, its capacity to move mountains (Matthew 17:20-21), heal sickness (Mark 10:52; Luke 7:50) and free individuals from anxiety (Matthew 6:28-30) dominates the teaching of Jesus. Most of all, faith overcomes fear. Jesus is repeatedly presented as the one whose very presence makes people unafraid. 'Take heart, it is I; have no fear' (Mark 6:50) and 'It is I; do not be afraid' (John 6:20) constitute one common thread linking John with the synoptics. In the fourth gospel, peace is the personal gift of the risen Christ to his disciples (John 14:27).

*

All things are possible to him who believes.   Mark 8:23

Let not your hearts be troubled; believe in God, believe also in me. In my Father's house are many rooms; if it were not so, would I have told you that I go to prepare a place for you?   John 14:1-2

Take heart, it is I; have no fear.   Mark 6:50

Man shall not live by bread alone, but by every word that proceeds from the mouth of God.   Matthew 4:4

Father, into thy hands I commit my spirit!   Luke 23:46

Peace I leave with you; my peace I give to you; not as the world gives do I give to you. Let not your hearts be troubled, neither let them be afraid.   John 14:27

When the Son of man comes will he find faith on earth?   Luke 18:8

Do not be anxious about tomorrow, for tomorrow will be anxious for itself. Let the day's own trouble be sufficient for the day.   Matthew 6:34

Believe me that I am in the Father and the Father in me; or else believe me for the sake of the works themselves.
                                                            John 14:11

[To the disciples] Where is your faith?   Luke 8:25

Blessed are those who have not seen and yet believe.
                                                            John 20:29

Consider the lilies of the field, how they grow; they neither toil nor spin; yet I tell you, even Solomon in all his glory was not arrayed like one of these. But if God so clothes the grass of the field, which today is alive and tomorrow is thrown into the oven, will he not much more clothe you, O men of little faith?   Matthew 6:28-30

If any one thirst, let him come to me and drink. He who believes in me, as the scripture has said, 'Out of his heart shall flow rivers of living water.'   John 7:37-38

I tell you, ask, and it will be given you; seek, and you will find; knock, and it will be opened to you.   Luke 11:9

Truly, truly, I say to you, he who believes has eternal life.
                                                            John 6:47

[To Thomas] Put your finger here, and see my hands; and put out your hand, and place it in my side; do not be faithless, but believing.   John 20:27

Take heart, daughter; your faith has made you well.
                                                            Matthew 9:22

Truly, truly, I say to you, he who believes in me will also do the works that I do; and greater works than these will he do, because I go to the Father.   John 14:12

Truly, truly, I say to you, one of you will betray me.
                                                            John 13:21

O faithless and perverse generation, how long am I to be with you? How long am I to bear with you?

Matthew 17:17

It is I; do not be afraid.

John 6:20

[To the sinful woman] Your faith has saved you; go in peace.

Luke 7:50

Who touched my garments? ... Daughter, your faith has made you well; go in peace and be healed of your disease.

Mark 5:31-34

Go your way; your faith has made you well.

Mark 10:52

Blessed rather are those who hear the word of God and keep it !

Luke 11:28

Truly, I say to you, whoever says to this mountain, 'Be taken up and cast into the sea,' and does not doubt in his heart, but believes that what he says will come to pass, it will be done for him.

Mark 11:24

For truly, I say to you, if you have faith as a grain of mustard seed, you will say to this mountain, 'Move from here to there,' and it will move; and nothing will be impossible to you.

Matthew 17:20-21

If you had faith as a grain of mustard seed, you could say to this sycamine tree, 'Be rooted up, and be planted in the sea,' and it would obey you.

Luke 17:6

[To Peter] Truly, I say to you, this very night, before the cock crows, you will deny me three times.

Matthew 26:34

Abba, Father, all things are possible to thee; remove this cup from me; yet not what I will, but what thou wilt.

Mark 14:36

He who is faithful in a very little is faithful also in much; and he who is dishonest in a very little is dishonest also in much.   Luke 16:10

[To the disciples] Why do you trouble this woman? For she has done a beautiful thing to me. For you always have the poor with you, but you will not always have me. In pouring this ointment on my body she has done it to prepare me for burial. Truly, I say to you, wherever this gospel is preached in the whole world, what she has done will be told in memory of her.   Matthew 26:10-13

Which of you by being anxious can add a cubit to his span of life?   Luke 12:25

Martha, Martha, you are anxious and troubled about many things; one thing is needful.   Luke 10:41

[Concerning the centurion] I tell you, not even in Israel have I found such faith.   Luke 7:9

[To the disciples in the storm] Why are you afraid? Have you no faith?   Mark 4:40

[To the disciples] Why do you discuss the fact that you have no bread? Do you not yet perceive or understand? Are your hearts hardened? Having eyes do you not see, and having ears do you not hear? And do you not remember? When I broke the five loaves for the five thousand, how many baskets full of broken pieces did you take up?   Mark 8:17-19

My God, my God, why hast thou forsaken me?
                                                        Mark 15:34

These signs will accompany those who believe: in my name they will cast out demons; they will speak in new tongues; they will pick up serpents, and if they drink any deadly thing, it will not hurt them; they will lay their hands on the sick, and they will recover.   Mark 16:17

[To Nathanael] Truly, truly, I say to you, you will see heaven opened, and the angels of God ascending and descending upon the Son of man.   John 1:50

While you have the light, believe in the light, that you may
become sons of light.   John 12:36

[On the road to Emmaus] O foolish men, and slow of heart
to believe all that the prophets have spoken! Was it not
necessary that the Christ should suffer these things and
enter into his glory?   Luke 24:25-26

What man of you, if his son asks him for bread, will give
him a stone? Or if he asks for a fish, will give him a
serpent? If you then, who are evil, know how to give good
gifts to your children, how much more will your Father
who is in heaven give good things to those who ask
him!   Matthew 6:9-11

[To the two blind men in need of healing] Do you believe
that I am able to do this? ... According to your faith be it
done to you.   Matthew 9:28-29

[To Peter trying to walk on water] O man of little faith, why
did you doubt?   Matthew 14:31

[To the disciples in the Garden of Gethsemane] Are you
still sleeping and taking your ease? Behold, the hour is at
hand, the Son of man is betrayed into the hands of
sinners.   Matthew 26:45

Love

Agapê – selfless love – is the 'new commandment' of Jesus (John 13:34). In fact it is only 'new' in the sense that *agapê* is conceived of as the centrally distinguishing mark of those who call themselves Christians: no love, no Christianity. John understands love as the dynamic of the inner relationship between the Father and the Son. 'As the Father has loved me, so have I loved you: abide in my love' (John 15:9). The community of the disciples is modelled therefore on the free, self-giving love of God – understood as Father and Son (and of course subsequently as Spirit). John envisages that loving relationships will be the criterion by which Christians will be known (13:35). By exhibiting love, Christians show that they are 'of ' another world, which is why the world will hate them (John 15:18-19). In the synoptics, the love of Christ takes precedence over the love of family. 'He who loves father or mother more than me is not worthy of me' (Matthew 10:37). The commandment to love one's enemies and pray for persecutors (Matthew 5:43-45) is probably the most radical aspect of the recorded teaching of Jesus – especially when one considers that the community which remembered and preserved these sayings was itself persecuted.

*

The Father himself loves you, because you have loved me and have believed that I came from the Father.

John 16:27

He who loves father or mother more than me is not worthy of me; and he who loves son or daughter more than me is not worthy of me; and he who does not take his cross and follow me is not worthy of me. He who finds his life will lose it, and he who loses his life for my sake will find it.

Matthew 10:37-39

For he whom God has sent utters the words of God, for it is not by measure that he gives the Spirit; the Father loves the Son, and has given all things into his hand.   John 3:34-35

Father, I desire that they also, whom thou hast given me, may be with me where I am, to behold my glory which thou hast given me in thy love for me before the foundation of the world.   John 17:24

You have heard that it was said, 'You shall love your neighbour and hate your enemy.' But I say to you, love your enemies and pray for those who persecute you, so that you may be sons of your Father who is in heaven.
     Matthew 5:43-45

If a man loves me, he will keep my word, and my Father will love him, and we will come to him and make our home with him.   John 14:23

The first commandment is, 'Hear O Israel; The Lord our God, the Lord is one; and you shall love the Lord your God with all your heart, and with all your soul, and with all your mind, and with all your strength.' The second is this, 'You shall love your neighbour as yourself.' There is no other commandment greater than these.   Mark 12:29-31

Simon, son of John, do you love me?   John 21:17

As the Father has loved me, so have I loved you; abide in my love. If you keep my commandments, you will abide in my love, just as I have kept my Father's commandments and abide in his love.   John 15:9-11

You search the scriptures, because you think that in them you have eternal life; and it is they that bear witness to me; yet you refuse to come to me that you may have life. I do not receive glory from men. But I know that you have not the love of God within you.   John 5:39-42

If the world hates you, know that it has hated me before it hated you. If you were of the world, the world would love its own; but because you are not of the world, but I chose you out of the world, therefore the world hates you.   John 15:18-19

If you love those who love you, what credit is that to you? For even sinners love those who love them. And if you do good to those who do good to you, what credit is that to you? For even sinners do the same. Luke 6:32-33

A new commandment I give to you, that you love one another; even as I have loved you, that you also love one another. By this all men will know that you are my disciples, if you have love for one another. John 13:34-35

If you love me, you will keep my commandments.
John 14:15

For the Father loves the Son, and shows him all that he himself is doing; and greater works than these will he show him, that you may marvel. John 5:20

For this reason the Father loves me, because I lay down my life, that I may take it again. No one takes it from me, but I lay it down of my own accord. I have power to lay it down, and I have power to take it again; this charge I have received from my Father. John 10:17-18

Greater love hath no man than this, that a man lay down his life for his friends. John 15:13

You did not choose me, but I chose you and appointed you that you should go and bear fruit and that your fruit should abide; so that whatever you ask the Father in my name, he may give it to you. This I command you, to love one another. John 15:16-17

Judgment

At least three kinds of judgment are encountered in the gospels. The first is the way in which Jesus is presented as opposing the religious of his day and their own hypocrisy and self-righteousness. The scribes and pharisees are charged with having followed the letter of the law but having neglected the 'weightier matters' of 'justice and mercy and faith' (Matthew 23:23). Whether as a reflection of later conflict or not, the evangelists present Jesus as not sparing them the severest condemnation (Matthew 23:27). The second is John's conception of Christ as the light that reveals the darkness of the human condition. 'Men loved darkness,' it is claimed, 'because their deeds were evil' (John 3:19). Judgment in this sense is continuous, inaugurated by the presence of the Son – not that judgment is the intention, rather that humans judge themselves by their failure to respond to the light presented to them (John 5:22-24; 9:39; 12:47-48). The third is the final judgment envisaged by the synoptics as the return of the Son of man. This is to be a day of tribulation and reckoning (Mark 13:24-27; Matthew 24:7-9; 29-31). It is interesting that the criterion of judgment in Matthew's famous parable of the end time turns out to be ethical and seems to depend little on faith as such. Only those who have fed the hungry, given water to the thirsty, welcomed strangers, visited prisoners and clothed the naked are to inherit the kingdom and escape final judgment (Matthew 25:31-36).

*

Woe to you that are rich, for you have received your consolation. Woe to you that are full now, for you shall hunger. Woe to you that laugh now, for you shall mourn and weep. Woe to you, when all men speak well of you, for so their fathers did to the false prophets.   Luke 6:24-26

Well did Isaiah prophesy of you hypocrites, as it is written, 'This people honours me with their lips, but their heart is far from me; in vain do they worship me, teaching as doctrines the precepts of men.' You leave the commandment of God, and hold fast the tradition of men.   Mark 7:6-8

This is the judgment, that the light has come into the world, and men loved darkness rather than light, because their deeds were evil.   John 3:19

Why do you see the speck that is in your brother's eye, but do not notice the log that is in your own eye?
                                                         Matthew 7:3

Judge not, that you be not judged.   Matthew 7:1

Judge not, and you will not be judged; condemn not, and you will not be condemned; forgive, and you will be forgiven; give, and it will be given to you; good measure, pressed down, shaken together, running over, will be put into your lap. For the measure you give will be the measure you get back.   Luke 6:37-39

But in those days, after that tribulation, the sun will be darkened, and the moon will not give its light, and the stars will be falling from heaven, and the powers in the heavens will be shaken. And then they will see the Son of man coming in clouds with great power and glory. And then he will send out the angels, and gather his elect from the four winds; from the ends of the earth to the ends of heaven.
                                                        Mark 13:24-27

Immediately after the tribulation of those days the sun will be darkened, and the moon will not give its light, and the stars will fall from heaven, and the powers of the heavens will be shaken; then will appear the sign of the Son of man in heaven, and then all the tribes of the earth will mourn, and they will see the Son of man coming on the clouds of heaven with power and great glory; and he will send out his angels with a loud trumpet call, and they will gather his elect from the four winds, from one end of heaven to the other.   Matthew 24:29-31

Would that even today you knew the things that make for peace! But now they are hid from your eyes. For the days shall come upon you, when your enemies will cast up a bank about you and surround you, and hem you in on every side, and dash you to the ground, you and your children within you, and they will not leave one stone upon another in you; because you did not know the time of your visitation. Luke 19:42-44

The Father judges no one, but has given all judgment to the Son, that all may honour the Son, even as they honour the Father. He who does not honour the Son does not honour the Father who sent him. John 5:22-23

Enter by the narrow gate; for the gate is wide and the way is easy that leads to destruction, and those who enter by it are many. For the gate is narrow and the way is hard, that leads to life, and those who find it are few.
Matthew 7:13-14

Strive to enter by the narrow door; for many, I tell you, will seek to enter and will not be able. Luke 13:24

For judgment I came into this world, that those who do not see may see, and that those who see may become blind.
John 9:39

Your eye is the lamp of your body; when your eye is sound, your whole body is full of light; but when it is not sound, your body is full of darkness. Therefore be careful lest the light in you be darkness. Luke 11:34-35

Woe to you, Chorazin! woe to you, Bethsaida! for if the mighty works done in you had been done in Tyre and Sidon, they would have repented long ago, sitting in sackcloth and ashes. But it shall be more tolerable in the judgment for Tyre and Sidon than for you. And you Capernaum, will you be exalted to heaven? You shall be brought down to Hades. Luke 10:13-15

Beware of false prophets, who come to you in sheep's clothing but inwardly are ravenous wolves. You will know them by their fruits. Matthew 7:15

This generation is an evil generation; it seeks a sign, but no sign shall be given to it except the sign of Jonah. For as Jonah became a sign to the men of Nineveh, so will the Son of man be to this generation.   Luke 11:29-30

If anyone hears my sayings and does not keep them, I do not judge him; for I did not come to judge the world but to save the world. He who rejects me and does not receive my sayings has a judge; the word that I have spoken will be his judge on the last day.   John 12:47-48

Every one who acknowledges me before men, I also will acknowledge before my Father who is in heaven; but whoever denies me before men, I also will deny before my Father who is in heaven.   Matthew 10:32-33

Truly, truly, I say to you, the hour is coming, and now is, when the dead will hear the voice of the Son of God, and those who hear will live. For as the Father has life in himself, so he has granted the Son also to have life in himself, and has given him authority to execute judgment, because he is the Son of man.   John 5:25-27

I came to cast fire upon the earth; and would that it were already kindled!   Luke 12:49

Do not think that I have come to bring peace on earth; I have not come to bring peace, but a sword. For I have come to set a man against his father, and a daughter against her mother, and a daughter-in-law against her mother-in-law; and a man's foes will be those of his own household.   Matthew 10:34-36

Do you think that I have come to give peace on earth? No, I tell you, but rather division.   Luke 12:51

I tell you, every one who acknowledges me before men, the Son of man also will acknowledge before the angels of God; but he who denies me before men will be denied before the angels of God.   Luke 12:8-9

Truly, truly, I say to you, he who hears my word and
believes him who sent me, has eternal life; he does not
come into judgment, but has passed from death to
life.
John 5:24

Of that day or that hour no one knows, not even the angels
in heaven, nor the Son, but only the Father. Take heed,
watch; for you do not know when the time will come.
Mark 13:32-33

I tell you, my friends, do not fear those who kill the body,
and after that have no more that they can do. But I will
warn you whom to fear: fear him who, after he has killed,
has power to cast into hell; yes, I tell you, fear him!
Luke 12:4-5

Woe to you, scribes and pharisees, hypocrites! for you tithe
mint and dill and cummin, and have neglected the
weightier matters of the law, justice and mercy and faith;
these you ought to have done, without neglecting the
others.
Matthew 23:23

Woe to you, pharisees! for you tithe mint and rue and
every herb, and neglect justice and the love of God.
Luke 11:42

For the Son of man goes as it is written of him, but woe to
that man by whom the Son of man is betrayed! It would
have been better for that man if he had not been born.
Mark 14:21

Woe to you, scribes and pharisees, hypocrites! for you are
like white-washed tombs, which outwardly appear
beautiful, but within they are full of dead men's bones and
all uncleanness. So you also outwardly appear righteous to
men, but within you are full of hypocrisy and iniquity.
Matthew 23:27

Now you pharisees cleanse the outside of the cup and of
the dish, but inside you are full of extortion and
wickedness.
Luke 11:39

O Jerusalem, Jerusalem, killing the prophets and stoning those who are sent to you! How often would I have gathered your children together as a hen gathers her brood under her wings, and you would not! Behold, your house is forsaken and desolate.   Matthew 23:37-38

Watch therefore – for you do not know when the master of the house will come, in the evening, or at midnight, or at cockcrow, or in the morning – lest he come suddenly and find you asleep. And what I say to you I say to all: Watch.   Mark 13:35-37

When you hear of wars and rumours of wars, do not be alarmed; this must take place, but the end is not yet. For nation will rise against nation, and kingdom against kingdom; there will be earthquakes in various places, there will be famines; this is but the beginning of the birth-pangs.   Mark 13:7-8

For nation will rise against nation, and kingdom against kingdom, and there will be famines and earthquakes in various places: all this is but the beginning of the birth-pangs. Then they will deliver you up to tribulation, and put you to death; and you will be hated by all nations for my name's sake.   Matthew 24:7-9

Take heed to yourselves lest your hearts be weighed down with dissipation and drunkenness and cares of this life, and that day come upon you suddenly like a snare; for it will come upon all who dwell upon the face of the whole earth.   Luke 21:34-35

Daughters of Jerusalem, do not weep for me, but weep for yourselves and for your children. For behold, the days are coming when they will say 'Blessed are the barren, and the wombs that never bore, and the breasts that never gave suck!'   Luke 23:28-29

When the Son of man comes in his glory, and all the angels with him, then he will sit on his glorious throne. Before him will be gathered all the nations, and he will separate them one from another as a shepherd separates the sheep from the goats, and he will place the sheep at his right hand, but the goats at the left. Then the King will say to those at his right hand, 'Come, O blessed of my Father, inherit the kingdom prepared for you from the foundation of the world; for I was hungry and you gave me food, I was thirsty and you gave me drink, I was a stranger and you welcomed me, I was naked and you clothed me, I was sick and you visited me, I was in prison and you came to me.'

Matthew 25:31-36

[To the disciples] I tell you the truth: it is to your advantage that I go away, for if I do not go away, the Counsellor will not come to you; but if I go, I will send him to you. And when he comes, he will convince the world concerning sin, because they do not believe in me; concerning righteousness, because I go to the Father, and you will see me no more; concerning judgment, because the ruler of this world is judged.

John 16:7-11

Why do you not judge for yourselves what is right?

Luke 12:57

[Concerning the destruction of the Temple] Do you see these great buildings? There will not be left here one stone upon another, that will not be thrown down.   Mark 13:2

[To his mother] O woman, what have you to do with me? My hour has not yet come.

John 2:4

For every one who does evil hates the light, and does not come to the light, lest his deeds should be exposed. But he who does what is true comes to the light, that it may be clearly seen that his deeds have been wrought in God.

John 3:20

Do not think that I shall accuse you to the Father; it is Moses who accuses you, on whom you set your hope. If you believed Moses, you would believe me, for he wrote of me. But if you do not believe his writings, how will you believe my words?

John 5:45-47

You are those [pharisees who loved money] who justify yourselves; for what is exalted among men is an abomination in the sight of God.

Luke 16:15

You brood of vipers! how can you speak good, when you are evil? For out of the abundance of the heart the mouth speaks. The good man out of his good treasure brings forth good, and the evil man out of his evil treasure brings forth evil. I tell you, on the day of judgment men will render account for every careless word they utter; for by your words you will be justified, and by your words you will be condemned.   Matthew 12:34-37

When the unclean spirit has gone out of a man, he passes through the waterless places seeking rest, but he finds none. Then he says, 'I will return to my house from which I came.' And when he comes he finds it empty, swept and put in order. Then he goes and brings with him seven other spirits more evil than himself, and they enter and dwell there; and the last state of that man becomes worse than the first. So shall it be also with this evil generation.
                                                  Matthew 12:43-45

But of that day and hour no one knows, not even the angels of heaven, nor the Son, but the Father only.
                                                  Matthew 24:36

Salvation

The differences of emphasis between the synoptics and John seem most acute concerning the nature and scope of salvation. Luke, for example, identifies Jesus at the beginning of his ministry as the fulfilment of the messianic prophecy in Isaiah. The messiah is the one anointed by the Spirit to preach good news to the poor, release to the captives, recovery of sight to the blind, and to set at liberty those who are oppressed (4:18-19). From this perspective, salvation consists in the confession of Jesus as messiah, whose kingdom involves, not the rejection of the world, but its transformation and redemption. John, in contrast, seems to present Jesus as the personal saviour only of those who believe in him (6:40; 8:51; 17:38). These 'this-worldly' and 'other-worldly' emphases, however, are probably in tension to some degree within each gospel since eternal life is understood variously either as a condition of the present time (John 10:27-28) or as its fulfilment in another (Luke 18:29).

*

For God so loved the world that he gave his only Son, that whoever believes in him should not perish but have eternal life. For God sent the Son into the world, not to condemn the world, but that the world might be saved through him.

John 3:16-17

Today salvation has come to this house, since he [Zacchaeus, the repentant sinner] also is a son of Abraham. For the Son of man came to seek and to save the lost.

Luke 19:9-10

With men it [salvation] is impossible, but not with God; for all things are possible with God.   Mark 10:27

I am the resurrection and the life; he who believes in me, though he die, yet shall he live, and whoever lives and believes in me shall never die. John 11:25-26

Brother will deliver up brother to death, and the father his child, and children will rise against parents and have them put to death; and you will be hated by all for my name's sake. But he who endures to the end will be saved.
Matthew 10:21-22

For this is the will of my Father, that every one who sees the Son and believes in him should have eternal life; and I will raise him up at the last day. John 6:40

'The Spirit of the Lord is upon me, because he has anointed me to preach good news to the poor. He has sent me to proclaim release to the captives and recovering of sight to the blind, to set at liberty those who are oppressed, to proclaim the acceptable year of the Lord' ... Today this scripture has been fulfilled in your hearing.
Luke 4:18-19, 21

And every one who has left houses or brothers or sisters or father or mother or children or lands, for my name's sake, will receive a hundred-fold, and inherit eternal life. But many that are first will be last, and the last first.
Matthew 19:29-30

Truly, I say to you [criminal on the cross] today you will be with me in Paradise. Luke 23:43

Truly, truly, I say to you, if any one keeps my word, he will never see death. John 8:51

The cup that I drink you will drink; and with the baptism with which I am baptized, you will be baptized; but to sit at my right hand or at my left is not mine to grant, but it is for those for whom it has been prepared. Mark 10:39-40

This is eternal life, that they know thee the only true God, and Jesus Christ whom thou hast sent. John 17:3

Truly, I say to you, there is no man who has left house or
wife or brothers or parents or children, for the sake of the
kingdom of God, who will not receive manifold more in
this time, and in the age to come eternal life.

Luke 18:29-30

My sheep hear my voice, and I know them, and they follow
me; and I give them eternal life, and they shall never
perish, and no one shall snatch them out of my
hand.

John 10:27-28

The sons of this age marry and are given in marriage; but
those who are accounted worthy to attain to that age and to
the resurrection from the dead neither marry nor are given
in marriage, for they cannot die any more, because they are
equal to angels and are sons of God, being sons of the
resurrection. But that the dead are raised, even Moses
showed, in the passage about the bush, where he calls the
Lord the God of Abraham and the God of Isaac and the
God of Jacob. Now he is not God of the dead, but of the
living; for all live to him.

Luke 20:34-38

There will be signs in sun and moon and stars, and upon
the earth distress of nations in perplexity at the roaring of
the sea and the waves, men fainting with fear and with
foreboding of what is coming on the world; for the powers
of the heavens will be shaken. And then they will see the
Son of man coming in a cloud with power and great glory.
Now when these things begin to take place, look up and
raise your heads, because your redemption is drawing
near.

Luke 21:25-28

Truly, truly, I say to you, unless you eat the flesh of the Son
of man and drink his blood, you have no life in you; he
who eats my flesh and drinks my blood has eternal life, and
I will raise him up at the last day.

John 6:53-54

If a man has a hundred sheep, and one of them has gone
astray, does he not leave the ninety-nine on the mountains
and go in search of the one that went astray? And if he
finds it, truly, I say to you, he rejoices over it more than
over the ninety-nine that never went astray. So it is not the
will of my Father who is in heaven that one of these little
ones should perish.

Matthew 18:12-14

Truly, truly, I say to you, you will weep and lament, but the world will rejoice; you will be sorrowful, but your sorrow will turn into joy. When a woman is in travail she has sorrow, because her hour has come; but when she is delivered of the child, she no longer remembers the anguish, for joy that a child is born into the world. So you have sorrow now, but I will see you again and your hearts will rejoice, and no one will take your joy from you.

John 16:20-23

As Moses lifted up the serpent in the wilderness, so must the Son of man be lifted up, that whoever believes in him may have eternal life.   John 3:14-15

Whoever drinks of the water that I shall give him will never thirst; the water that I shall give him will become in him a spring of water welling up to eternal life.   John 3:14

Even the hairs of your head are numbered.

Matthew 10:30

Disclosure

'Who do men say that I am?' (Mark 8:29) is the underlying question of all four gospels. But the gospels provide no unified answer to this question. The reason for this seems to be that each gospel draws at least in part upon different strands of Christological reflection. There is no one doctrine of Jesus. The sayings of Jesus themselves reflect various stages of theological reflection and sophistication among those who remembered and transmitted them. In the synoptics, the person of Jesus is interpreted widely in terms of an eschatological figure, namely the Son of man (Mark 2:27-28; 9:31; Matthew 8:20; Luke 22:67-69, etc.) but its precise meaning is obscure. In John, various metaphors are used, including Jesus as 'the way, the truth and the life' (14:6); 'the bread of life' (6:35); 'the light of the world' (8:12) and 'the true vine' (15:1-2). Hardly anything of Jesus' own personal life and circumstances is revealed by his sayings. Who Jesus is and what his life means can only be tested in the last resort through experience. This is the explicit claim in John: If any one wishes to do God's will, 'he shall know whether the teaching is from God or whether I am speaking on my own authority' (7:16-17).

*

I am the way, and the truth, and the life; no one comes to the Father, but by me.   John 14:6

Go and tell John what you have seen and heard; the blind receive their sight, the lame walk, lepers are cleansed, and the deaf hear, the dead are raised up, the poor have good news preached to them. And blessed is he who takes no offence at me.   Luke 7:22

Foxes have holes, and birds of the air have nests; but the Son of man has nowhere to lay his head.   Matthew 8:20

My teaching is not mine, but his who sent me; if any man's will is to do his will, he shall know whether the teaching is from God or whether I am speaking on my own authority. John 7:16-17

The sabbath was made for man, not man for the sabbath; so the Son of man is lord even of the sabbath. Mark 2:27-28

[To Peter] But who do you say that I am? Luke 9:20

Father, I thank thee that thou hast heard me. I knew that thou hearest me always, but I have said this on account of the people standing by that they may believe that thou didst send me. John 11:41-42

Why do you call me good? No one is good but God alone. Luke 18:19

A prophet is not without honour except in his own country and in his own house. Matthew 13:57

All things have been delivered to me by my Father; and no one knows who the Son is except the Father, or who the Father is except the Son and any one to whom the Son chooses to reveal him. Luke 10:22

I am the light of the world; he who follows me will not walk in darkness, but will have the light of life. John 8:12

It is finished. John 19:30

The Son of man will be delivered into the hands of men, and they will kill him; and when he is killed, after three days he will rise. Mark 9:31

Truly, truly, I say to you, before Abraham was, I am. John 8:58

I thirst. John 19:28

If I tell you [the chief priests] you will not believe; and if I ask you, you will not answer. But from now on the Son of man shall be seated at the right hand of the power of God. Luke 22:67-69

My Father is working still, and I am working.   John 5:17

Truly, I say to you, as you did it to one of the least of these my brethren, you did it to me.   Matthew 25:40

I have yet many things to say to you, but you cannot bear them now. When the Spirit of truth comes, he will guide you into all the truth; for he will not speak on his own authority, but whatever he hears he will speak, and he will declare to you the things that are to come.   John 16:12-13

This is my body which is given for you. Do this in remembrance of me ....This cup which is poured out for you is the new covenant in my blood.   Luke 22:19-20

I am the bread of life; he who comes to me shall not hunger, and he who believes in me shall never thirst.
          John 6:35

I am the bread of life. Your fathers ate the manna in the wilderness, and they died. This is the bread which comes down from heaven, that a man may eat of it and not die. I am the living bread which came down from heaven; if any one eats of this bread, he will live for ever; and the bread which I shall give for the life of the world is my flesh.
          John 6:48-51

The Counsellor, the Holy Spirit, whom the Father will send in my name, he will teach you all things, and bring to your remembrance all that I have said to you.   John 14:26

See my hands and my feet, that it is I myself; handle me and see; for a spirit has not flesh and bones as you see that I have.   Luke 24:39-40

I am [the Christ, the Son of the Blessed] and you will see the Son of man seated at the right hand of power, and coming with the clouds of heaven.   Mark 14:62

I am the true vine, and my Father is the vinedresser. Every branch of mine that bears no fruit, he takes away, and every branch that does bear fruit he prunes, that it may bear more fruit.   John 15:1-2

You [Pilate] say that I am a king. For this I was born, and for this I have come into the world, to bear witness to the truth. Every one who is of the truth hears my voice.

John 18:37

Judas, would you betray the Son of man with a kiss?

Luke 22:48

It is the spirit that gives life, the flesh is of no avail; the words that I have spoken to you are spirit and life.

John 6:63

Heaven and earth will pass away, but my words will not pass away.   Mark 13:31

Let these words sink into your ears; for the Son of man is to be delivered into the hands of men.   Luke 9:44

I thank thee, Father, Lord of heaven and earth, that thou hast hidden these things from the wise and understanding and revealed them to babes; yea, Father, for such was thy gracious will.   Matthew 11:25

[Concerning John the Baptist] What did you go out into the wilderness to behold? A reed shaken by the wind? Why then did you go out? To see a man clothed in soft raiment? Behold those who wear soft raiment are in kings' houses. Why then did you go out? To see a prophet? Yes, I tell you, and more than a prophet. This is he of whom it is written, 'Behold, I send my messenger before thy face, who shall prepare thy way before thee.'   Matthew 11:7-10

[To Mary Magdalen] Woman, why are you weeping?

John 20:15

I who speak to you am he [he who is called Christ].

John 4:26

I shall be with you a little longer, and then I go to him who sent me; you will seek me and you will not find me; where I am you cannot come.   John 7:33-35

For their sake I consecrate myself.   John 17:19

[To Pilate] You would have no power over me unless it had been given you from above; therefore he who delivered me to you has the greater sin. John 19:11

[To Peter who thought that the Christ should not suffer] Get behind me, Satan! You are a hindrance to me; for you are not on the side of God, but of men. Matthew 16:23

[To the disciples after the resurrection] Do not be afraid; go and tell my brethren to go to Galilee, and there they will see me. Matthew 28:10

He [John the Baptist] was a burning and shining lamp, and you were willing to rejoice for a while in his light. But the testimony which I have is greater than that of John; for the works which the Father has granted me to accomplish, these very works which I am doing, bear witness that the Father has sent me. John 5:35-37

[To those seeking to stone him] I have shown you many good works from the Father; for which of these do you stone me? John 10:31-32

Some one touched me; for I perceive that power has gone forth from me. Luke 8:46

He who is of God hears the words of God; the reason why you do not hear them is that you are not of God. John 8:47

My food is to do the will of him who sent me, and to accomplish his work. Do you not say, 'There are yet four months, then comes the harvest?' I tell you, lift up your eyes, and see how the fields are already white for harvest. He who reaps receives wages, and gathers fruit for eternal life, so that sower and reaper may rejoice together. John 4:34-38

Truly, I say to you, in the new world, when the Son of Man shall sit on his glorious throne, you who have followed me will also sit on twelve thrones, judging the twelve tribes of Israel. Matthew 19:28

I am the good shepherd. The good shepherd lays down his
life for the sheep.   John 10:11

Truly, Truly, I say to you, the Son can do nothing of his
own accord, but only what he sees the Father doing; for
whatever he does, that the Son does likewise.

John 5:19

He who hears you [Jesus' disciples] hears me, and he who
rejects you rejects me, and he who rejects me rejects him
who sent me.   Luke 10:16